PYTHON CRASH COURSE:

5 Fundamental Skills to Learn and Apply Python Quickly Even for Total Beginners

JASON SCRATCH

Table of Contents

Introduction

The Python programming language would be really a contemporary online programming language that was originally conceived and made by Guido Rossum in 1980s. Since that moment, Python has become a high heeled programming language that is modular and adaptive. A variety of the biggest sites in the world are using Python, such as YouTube, Disqus, and Reddit. Python presents several attributes which make it an attractive programming platform such as stability, portability, object-oriented improvement, a strong standard library, and a wealth of third-party modules or bundles.

Stability Python was under active development since the late 1980s and is now thought to be a programming language. The programmers of this Python language conduct comprehensive functionality and regression testing to ensure the language stays bug-free and steady with every new release. Portability Python programming provides several features that make it an attractive option for online software development. Python programs are portable as Python interpreters are easily available for many modern operating systems together with some embedded computing applications. Object-oriented improvement the object-oriented nature of Python makes it the greatest initial language for new developers and simple to learn for programmers migrating to Python from additional object-oriented languages.

Python programming is instinctive and reinforces great application structure and object-oriented approaches. Standard library the standard Python library provides developers various attributes like more complex languages such as c++ while maintaining pragmatic and simple language syntax. Comprehensive file-based i/o, database interactivity, innovative exception handling and a slew of built-in data types make Python appropriate for both web programs and mimicked programming. This makes Python net programming a simple endeavor for program developers hoping to transition into net software development.

Third-party modules Python is famous to be an inclusive language utilizing extensive functionality inside the library. On the other hand, the growing prevalence of Python programming has caused a massive group of third-party packages modules or modules therefore that expand Python's functionality and permit the language to look after programming challenges which are exceptional. For example, modules can be obtained for managing non-standard database links and advanced cryptography functionality. Furthermore, there are modules available for managing everyday tasks such as reading record metadata, which include graphs, and compiling Python applications to standardized executable applications.

Python web programming has been made accessible as a consequence of accessibility to several web-centric modules to manage tasks like email, preserving http country, interacting with all JavaScript, along with other ordinary web development tasks.

The information evaluation procedure: 5 steps to enhance decision making

You need greater information analysis. With the ideal information analysis procedure and resources, what was an overwhelming quantity of disparate data becomes an easy, clear decision stage.

To boost your information evaluation skills and simplify your decisions, implement these five measures on your data evaluation procedure:

Step 1: establish your queries

On your organizational or business information evaluation, you have to start with the ideal query (s). Questions must be quantifiable, concise and clear. Layout your queries to qualify or disqualify prospective answers to your particular issue or opportunity.

As an example, begin with a clearly defined issue: a government contractor is currently experiencing increasing prices and is no more able to publish competitive contract tips. Among the several questions to figure out this business problem would comprise: could the firm reduce its employees without compromising quality?

Step 2: establish clear measurement priorities

This step divides to 2 sub-steps: a) pick what to quantify, and b) decide on how to quantify it.

A) pick what to quantify

Employing the authority's contractor instance, consider what type of information you would want to answer your main question. In cases like this, you'd want to understand the quantity and price of present employees and the proportion of time that they spend on essential business purposes.

In answering this query, you probably will need to answer several sub-questions (e.g.) are employees presently under-utilized? If this is so, what procedure developments could help?). At length, on your choice about which to measure, make certain to incorporate any sensible understanding any stakeholders may possess (e.g., if employees are decreased, how do the firm react to surges in demand?).

B) pick how to quantify it

Thinking about the way you quantify your information is equally as important, particularly prior to the information collection period, as your measuring procedure either backs up or discredits your investigation in the future. Crucial questions to ask to this measure include:

- What's your timeframe? (e.g., yearly versus quarterly prices)

- What is your unit of measure? (e.g., USD vs euro)

- What variables must be included? (e.g., only annual salary versus yearly salary and cost of personnel benefits)

Step 3: collect data

Together with your query clearly defined along with your measurement priorities place, now it is time to gather your own data. As you gather and organize your information, don't forget to keep these important points in mind:

- Before you gather new information, determine what data can be gathered from existing sources or databases available. Collect this information.

- Decide on a document saving and naming system beforehand to aid all tasked staff members collaborate. This procedure saves time and prevents staff members out of collecting the identical data twice.

- Should you have to assemble data via interviews or observation, then create a meeting template beforehand to guarantee consistency and conserve time.

- Maintain your gathered data organized within a log together with set dates and include some other origin notes as you proceed (like any information normalization done). This clinic divides your decisions in the future.

Step 4: analyse data

After you have gathered the ideal information to reply your query from step 1, it is time for deeper information analysis. Start by manipulating your information in several of unique ways, like hammering out it and discovering correlations or simply by making a pivot table in excel. A vanity enables you to filter and sort information from different factors and permits you to figure out the mean, maximum, minimum and standard deviation of your information -- only make sure you prevent those five dangers of statistical information analysis.

As you control information, you might find you've got the precise information you require, but more inclined, you may have to update your initial query or collect additional information. In any event, this original investigation of trends, correlations, variants along with outliers will help you concentrate your information evaluation on better replying your query and some other objections others may have.

Through this period, information analysis tools and applications are very beneficial. Visio, both Minitab and stata are excellent software packages for complex statistical data evaluation. But, generally, nothing really compares to Microsoft excel concerning decision-making tools. Should you require a a primer on each of the purposes excel accomplishes your information analysis, we advise this Harvard business course.

Step 5: allergic effects

After assessing your information and maybe conducting additional research, it is now time to translate your results. As you translate your investigation, remember which you can't ever establish a theory correct: instead, it's possible just to don't reject the hypothesis. Meaning no matter how much information you collect; opportunity could always hinder your own results.

As you translate the outcome of your information, inquire these critical questions:

- Can the information answer your initial question? How?

- Can the information enable you to defend against any conscience? How?

- Can there be some limit in your decisions, any angles that you have not considered?

If the interpretation of this information holds up under all these questions and concerns, then you probably have come into a successful decision. The only remaining step is to utilize the outcomes of your data evaluation procedure to determine your very best strategy.

By following these five measures on your information analysis procedure, you create better choices for your business enterprise or government service as your decisions are backed by information that's been robustly accumulated and examined. With training, your information analysis gets quicker and more precise -- meaning that you create better, more educated decisions to conduct your business effectively.

Chapter 1 Evolution of Python

The Origins and Evolution of Python Language

Since its inception, Python has been designed to make available to the most significant number, a simple and intuitive development tool for creating scripts.

The Meeting between Python and Data Science

The emergence of data science is recent, and these new uses of data have often had difficulty finding suitable tools. Indeed, the data scientist must be a good developer while remaining a good data analyst. He has had to opt for a tool that would combine this demand with more and more strong development and automation (all the more so with the arrival of artificial intelligence and connected objects), with the need for a toolbox suitable for data applications.

Many avenues have been explored, in particular with the software R which continues to be a reference in data science but that could seem too oriented towards statistics for more developmentally oriented data scientists.

History, Origins and Evolution: From Birth to Version 3.717

Many other tools for setting up data science processes have been developed (most proprietors such as Matlab or SAS), but it turns out that Python (which combines powerful language and extremely simple) has managed to draw its pin.

The first real advance was the creation of NumPy (Numerical Python) package, which is still today the cornerstone of the Python ecosystem for data science. On the other hand, setting up data-driven Python environments with Anaconda has also enabled a whole community to come together around Python and data. Finally, IPython and its notebooks (now Jupyter) have completed the ecosystem to provide data scientists with a straightforward language but one which is extremely comprehensive for data science. This global environment resulted in the development of many packages and APIs, which today make Python the best tool to automate data science treatments.

The Current Evolution

In recent years, Python has taken an essential place in the world of data processing. While in the early 2010s, it seemed clear that in the world of open-source data processing tools, the software R was going to carve out the lion's share, a significant change has taken place since a few years. The emergence of Python as a language related to data science, machine learning, deep learning, and artificial intelligence is speedy.

Grace, an extremely active community under the PyData banner and frequent and numerous events (PyCon, PyData, JupyterCon, SciPyCon ...), language development took an unexpected turn. While we could hear in 2015 developers say that from machine learning the development of Python was modeled on that of R with a few months late. Today, it is R who begins to model his developments in the field of machine learning, deep learning, and big data, on packages developed in Python. In 2018, KDnuggets, an influential blog in the world of data science, even surveyed thousands of data scientists around the world. The latter, for the first time, and showed more users of Python than of R.

The Python adventure in data science is therefore recent but only because it is a language that adapts perfectly to the approach led by a data scientist, which would be: "better in programming than a statistician and better in statistics than a developer. "

The Future of Python

The near future of Python is above all the abandonment of version 2 and the generic version 3. The other significant current development concerns the use of interactive interfaces with Python as a communication language with more and more advanced APIs. We'll talk a little bit further about Jupyter's widgets that allow you to develop interactively and build interfaces in a few lines.

Python is increasingly used as a language to communicate with other environments. So Python can communicate with Apache Spark through PySpark medium, or with deep learning ecosystems such as TensorFlow. Calculations are no longer done in the Python engine but much more in engine devices using distributed infrastructures or GPU-based computations (Graphical Process Units). This trend is only beginning with the massification of data and requests for real-time treatments are ever more common.

Python can not answer these challenges alone but, combined with other tools, it allows the data scientist to manage the entire ecosystem of data processing, be it big, small, smart...

Python vs R vs. The Rest of the World

If you read this book, you must have heard about other tools in data science. Today we find an extremely developed ecosystem in this domain with languages such as R and Python but also more software like Dataiku DSS, IBM-SPSS Modeler, Enterprise Miner SAS, Azure machine learning from Microsoft ... As a data scientist, you can be brought to cross some of these tools in your missions. It is therefore vital to understand where everyone's strength lies.

We focus here on Python and its use by data scientists. So why is Python gaining ground on the competition?

In recent years, the global trend has shifted towards more code in the processing process and Python responds correctly to this request. Thus, the data scientist tools are increasingly different from those of the BI analyst (business intelligence) which are more and more intuitive. In this context, two open-source tools take the lead: Python and R.

Regarding proprietary tools, a trend is becoming widespread. This is the use of languages such as Python or R inside these tools as soon as we need to perform complex operations. So Dataiku DSS, RapidMiner or KNIME integrate modules to develop in Python or R. Your skills in Python will, therefore, be valued as part of the use of these tools.

R

R and Python are today the indispensable bases of the data scientist. Furthermore, the rapid evolution of both languages leads to a form of healthy competition making them more and more complete for data processing. However, some notable differences will guide your choices of the language decision to use for a project.

R is based on a language created for statisticians by statisticians, it is first and foremost on a descriptive and data modeling approach. The R outputs are outputs worthy of "classic" statistical software with many details. Python is not based on this approach, it's a language of programming to automate processes by just looking to calculate the bare minimum. As part of the current approaches to data application science, Python is more adapted to other needs than R.

On the other hand, Python is an elementary programming language based on a very readable syntax. Its understanding by many users is facilitated, which allows for better interaction between the different professions related to information systems (managers, developers, data scientists, data engineers ...).

To summarize, Python is the language of automation that integrates perfectly within a broader IT service framework and which adapts to the contexts of artificial intelligence (unstructured data, complex environments). It stays nevertheless lower than R for a statistician looking for statistical software.

R and Python are complementary today and will be very necessary for you frequently for your treatments.

Python's license is a "classic" free license, it allows you to reuse source code, modify it, market it, and to make all use without obligation to open your code. This is the type of license conventionally used for programming languages. All the Python ecosystem for data is based on this license. On the other hand, R is based on a more restrictive license, this is the GPL v3 license. This one gives responsibilities to the development community.

Indeed, if you use source code R and modify it to distribute it, you will be forced to make this code accessible to users (open source). Going again further, this license is "contaminating", that is, if you embed code licensed to your code, your code is licensed and must be open source. This point can frighten some developers who sometimes turn to Python. This difference between the two languages that are R and Python translates a difference of language development between the two communities. R developers are more in an idea to "force" advanced users to contribute to the project and Python developers are betting on an extensive use of the language that draws more contributions for language development.

Flow Processing Tools

The other tools of data science are for the most part facilitators, so the majority of these tools are based on Dataiku, RapidMiner's DSS flow creation (KNIME, IBM-SPSS Modeler ...) using your mouse. They simplify the life of the users and, depending on your needs, can save you time. However, everything these tools can do can be done directly with Python and they all incorporate ways to add Python code to streams.

These tools will allow you to create analyzes, from acquisition to analysis of data in a few clicks. For example, you can go for data in different formats at a first level, check and merge these data to the following level, transform the data, cut them out and apply and validate predictive models on these data. All this is included in a single stream.

Python will be very different from this visual treatment but will be able to reproduce this type of stream as a code. Moreover, as soon as bricks of your treatments become more complex, the use of Python inside each brick becomes necessary.

SAS

We will dwell here on a specific point because it concerns many users in the professional world. For some time now, many companies decided to migrate their infrastructures from SAS history to new languages (R and Python). It may be helpful to clarify a few points about this.

SAS is a proprietary software specialized in data processing. It accumulates nearly forty years of experience in this field and can not be replaced easily. Companies have often relied on this tool for the processing of their data. Nevertheless, moving to a tool like Python can be justified for several reasons:

From an economic point of view: this is often the first reason given. SAS licenses are costly. But the change will also be expensive, it requires changing the ways of working and more exceptional support for infrastructure than before.

From a technological point of view: this is the most essential point. The transition to Python will provide access to much more powerful machine learning, deep learning, and unstructured data processing methods than with SAS.

It should be kept in mind that this change will lead to several advantages. Mainly the fact that Python is a language that will load the data in memory in your machine while SAS was using an intermediate system of tables stored on physical memory. You will need to change your study and go through more sophisticated queries to your databases. Then, the processing and analyzing process will be largely simplified.

Python will, therefore, provide you with significant flexibility. Still, you will have to modify your approach to data management and code development with Python.

Other Languages

We compared Python to data science tools but another exciting comparison can be being compared to other programming languages. Today many languages are available. We can cite so many from the data universe: Julia, MatLab, C / C ++, Scala. These languages all have their specificities; we can classify them into two categories:

Interpreted languages such as MatLab, Julia, and Scala are credible alternatives to Python in a data science-oriented framework.

How to Develop In Python?

Compiled languages such as C, C ++, Java that fall into another category and are aimed at more experienced developers. In some cases, they are more efficient than Python. Still, they do not have a package and API environment as developed as Python.

Chapter 2 Introduction to Python

What Is Python?

Python, created in 1990 by Guido van Rossu, is a general-purpose, high-level programming language. It has become trendy over the past decade, thanks to its intuitive nature, flexibility, and versatility. Python can be used on a wide variety of operating systems. Its clean, readable code style makes it relatively beginner-friendly, while not as fast as other languages, such as C++ or JAVA, Python code is often much shorter and simpler than other languages.

Python also supports several packages and modules created by other developers to make the development of Python applications quicker and easier.

Why Learn Python?

There are hundreds of different programming languages out there in the world, with Wikipedia listing over 700 notable languages. Given how many languages you could potentially learn, why learn Python?

Python has seen an explosion in popularity in recent years, driven by several aspects that make it an incredibly versatile and intuitive language. A huge selling point of Python is the cleanliness and readability of its syntax and structure. Commands in Python can often

24

be carried out using simple English keywords, which makes the language much more intuitive than many other languages. Python is also quite versatile in the sense that it supports both structured programming and object-oriented programming approaches. Python even allows the use of certain aspects of functional programming.

Python is supported by many different operating systems, including Windows, Mac, and Linux platforms. Since Python is an interpreted programming language, Python programs can be run on multiple platforms without being recompiled.

Python comes with a robust standard library of modules, functions, and tools. Every module that comes with Python is a powerful tool you can use without creating additional code. Python comes pre-packaged with modules that assist in the creation of various web services, manipulating strings, and working with the operating system's interface. Python also makes it easy for users to create their libraries and frameworks, meaning that there is a large, open-source Python community continually creating a wide variety of applications. These applications can significantly speed up/simplify the development of your application.

Despite its simplicity, Python is also sturdy and robust enough to carry out sophisticated scientific and mathematical tasks. Python has been designed with features that drastically simplify the visualization and analysis of data, and Python is also the go-to choice for the creation of machine learning models and artificial intelligence.

For all of these reasons, Python is one of the fastest-growing and most in-demand computer programming skills.

A Note on Python Versions

There are various versions of Python available for use. It is highly recommended that you use version 3.7 or advanced when following along with this book. While Python 2 remains popular in some communities, support for Python 2 will end in 2020, meaning that security issues will not be resolved, and additional improvements won't be made to it. Once Python 2 is officially retired, only Python 3.5 and advanced will see continued support. Python 2's syntax is a little different from Python 3's syntax, and this will not teach Python 2 because its retirement is impending.

Definitions: Interpreter, Terminal, Shell, IDE

Early on in this book, and as you continue to program with Python, you will see many references to concepts like "interpreter," "terminal," "shell," and "IDE." These concepts can be somewhat confusing for a beginner, so to make things simpler, let's define these concepts here. If you are already somewhat familiar with these programming concepts and just looking to learn Python as another language, feel free to skip this section.

An "interpreter" in the computer science/programming sense is a computer program that can execute code, carrying out the written instructions specified by a programming or scripting language. An interpreter carries out code immediately and directly. In contrast, a "compiler" is a program that translates instructions into efficient machine code. Meanwhile, a "shell" is a wrapper or environment whose primary function is to run other programs and the word shell is often used to refer to the command-line of the OS. The command line takes in commands centered on the name of applications the user wishes to interact with. The interface you see above is an example of the Python shell, and it is running an interpreter.

Python has its shell; an interactive interpreter specialized for running Python commands. It lets the user immediately execute Python code and see the result as soon as the user enters the command. The Python shell that can be accessed through the command-line is an example of a "terminal," which is simply the environment that allows the user to input text and receives outputs. For the purpose of this book, the terms "shell" and "terminal" may be used interchangeably in reference to an instance of the Python interpreter accessed through the command line.

The Python Interpreter

There are two main ways to work with Python: with the interpreter and command line or with an Integrated Development Environment (IDE).

We will be doing the majority of our programming in an IDE, but first, let's make sure you understand how to work with Python in the terminal.

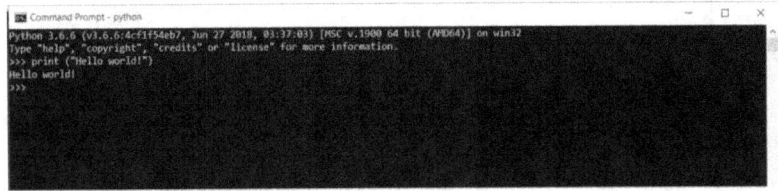

Let's start by opening the terminal/command prompt and checking that Python is installed correctly by just typing the command "python." If Python is properly installed, the command prompt should transition you to an instance of the Python interpreter/shell. This interpreter allows you to create and run Python code. For instance, if you copied this line of code into the terminal, you'd get "Using the terminal interpreter!" printed back out:

print ("Using the terminal interpreter!")

The command print() is responsible for printing out to the terminal whatever is specified inside the parentheses.

Most programming is done in an IDE, but it is still a good idea to learn how the Python interpreter works because there may be occasions where you may have to do some programming in it. With that in mind, let's take a few moments to familiarize ourselves with the Python interpreter.

As mentioned, the Python interpreter can typically be invoked from the command line only by entering the command "Python," or perhaps the specific Python version you want to run:

python3.8

The interpreter can typically be exited with the quit command: exit() - or depending on the version you are running - quit().

The help() command is an incredibly helpful command that you will always want to remember because it shows you all the various commands and functions that you can use in the interpreter.

When you enter a command by hitting the return key, the statement will be evaluated for correct syntax. If there is a syntax error, the error will be displayed.

Python is waiting for a command if you see the "primary prompt," which is often indicated by the presence of three greater-than signs (>>>). If you are on the second line of an input, these greater than signs will instead be replaced with three periods.

Using an IDE

I wanted to make you aware of the Python interpreter in the terminal's existence, but most of our programming will be done in an IDE. If you experimented with the terminal a little bit, you'd quickly find a significant disadvantage of using the terminal, and it is that you can't preserve many lines of code on the same screen. In addition, whenever you enter a line of code, and it contains any errors, a syntax error will be thrown immediately. IDEs make the process of learning a language simpler because they will often highlight syntax errors for you. Other benefits of using an IDE include auto-completion for specific key phrases and functions, more accessible collaboration with other programmers, and the ability to make changes to a script even while an instance of the programming is running.

You can try out the code examples found in this either the terminal or in an IDE. However, most of the examples presented in this will be presented in an IDE. One excellent IDE is PyCharm (https://www.jetbrains.com/pycharm), an open-source IDE designed from the ground up for use with Python. PyCharm highlights syntax errors enables easy refactoring/renaming of files and comes with an integrated debugger. PyCharm also has an integrated terminal, and when you run programs in PyCharm, the results of the program's execution will be displayed in the terminal at the bottom of the IDE.

Using PyCharm

Let's go over some of the functions in PyCharm in greater detail, so that you are familiar with how to use it.

After installing PyCharm and setting it up for the first time, you may be slightly intimidated by all the options, but don't worry, you won't be using most of these options for the exercises in this book.

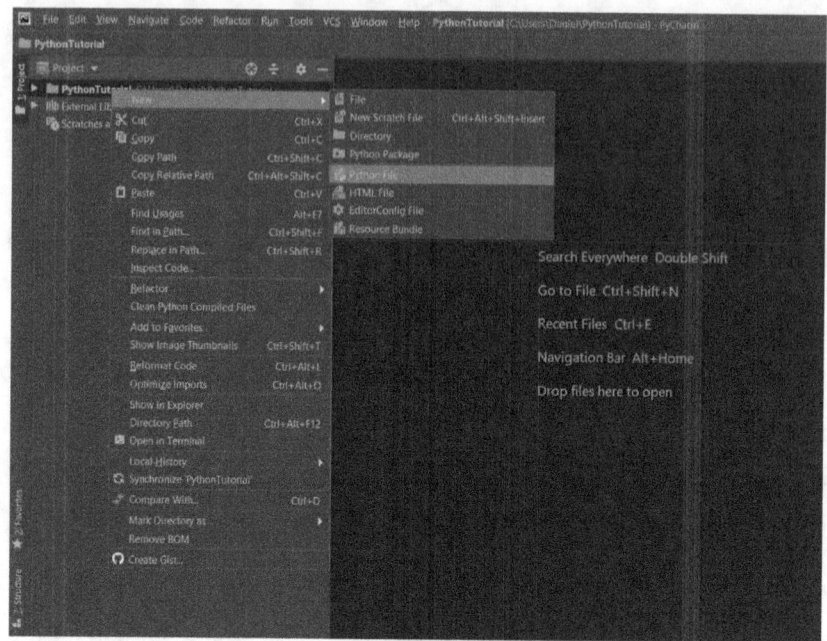

As you can see in the image above, when you open PyCharm and are confronted with the interface, you can navigate up to the file option in the top left corner. Opening the file drop-down menu will let you either open an existing project or create a new project. Opening an existing project enables you to reopen projects you've already started and saved or even open the projects that other people have worked on and which you have downloaded/cloned. For now, just create a new project for the exercises through the "File" option in the top left.

The New Project dialog box may look slightly different depending on which version of PyCharm you are using, but it should ask you to select a project interpreter. The default virtual environment (virtualenv) is beautiful for now, and it should automatically detect your base Python interpreter if it is correctly installed on your computer.

After this, you can create a folder to hold the scripts you create by right-clicking in the project frame and choosing the "New" option from the drop-down menu. To create a new Python script, just right-click on the folder you've created and navigate to "New" and then the "Python File" option. Now just enter a name for your new file Python file.

After you create a new Python file, it should automatically open in the editor panel to the right. You can now enter code into the editor. If, for some reason, the editor didn't automatically open the file, just double click on the file to open it up in the editor.

PyCharm should automatically save changes to the file, which means you don't need to worry about manually saving them. If for some reason, the file doesn't auto-save, or you just want to be sure it has saved, you can right-click on the file to be presented with a drop-down menu that should contain the option to save the file. You can also press Ctrl + S to save all the files currently open in PyCharm.

Once you've written some code and want to try running it, you can either navigate up to the "Run" tab on the top toolbar and select "Run (Current file name here)," or press Shift + F10. The image above shows a program has finished its run in PyCharm's compiler. Note that the results of the program are printed to the built-in terminal.

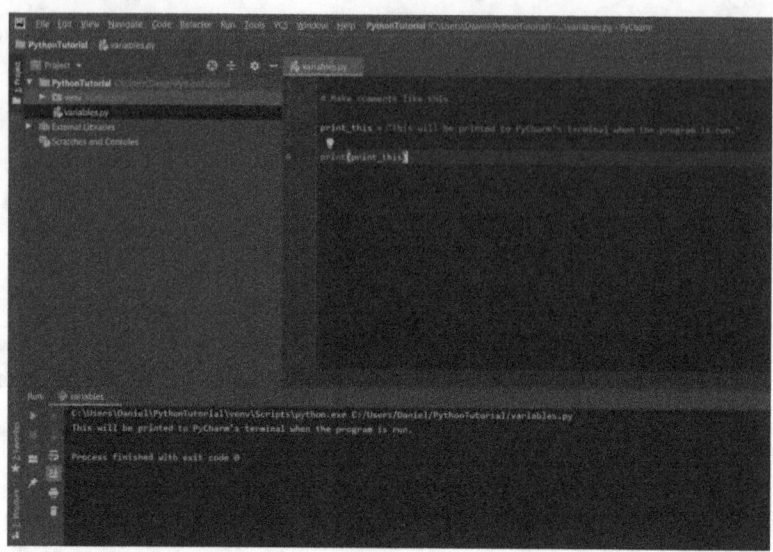

Chapter 3 Variables and Constants in Python:

What Is A Variable in Python?

When writing complex codes, your program will demand data essential to conduct changes when you proceed with your executions. Variables are, therefore, sections used to store code values created after you assign a value during program development. Python, unlike other related language programming software, lacks the command to declare a variable as they change after being set. Besides, Python values are undefined like in most cases of programming in other computer languages.

Variation in Python is therefore described as memory reserves used for storing data values. As such, Python variables act as storage units, which feed the computer with the necessary data for processing. Each value comprises of its database in Python programming, and every data is categorized as Numbers, Tuple, Dictionary and List, among others. As a programmer, you understand how variables work and how helpful they are in creating an effective program using Python. As such, the tutorial will enable learners to understand declare, re-declare, and concatenate, local and global variables as well as how to delete a variable.

Variable vs. Constants

Variables and constants are two components used in Python programming but perform separate functions. Variables, as well as constants, utilize values used to create codes to execute during program creation. Variables act as essential storage locations for data in the memory, while constants are variables whose value remains unchanged. In comparison, variables store reserves for data while constants are a type of variable files with consistent values written in capital letters and separated by underscores.

Variables vs. Literals

Variables also are part of literals which are raw data fed on either variable or constant with several literals used in Python programming. Some of the common types of literals used include Numeric, String, and Boolean, Special and Literal collections such as Tuple, Dict, List, and Set. The difference between variables and literals arises where both deal with unprocessed data but variables store the while laterals feeds the data to both constants and variables.

Variables vs. Arrays

Python variables have a unique feature where they only name the values and store them in the memory for quick retrieval and supplying the values when needed. On the other hand, Python arrays or collections are data types used in programming language and categorized into list, tuple, set, and dictionary, which will be later. When compared to variables, the array tends to provide a platform to include collectives functions when written while variables store all kinds of data intended. When choosing your charming collection, ensure you select the one that fits your requirements henceforth meaning retention of meaning, enhancing data security and efficiency.

Classifications of Python Arrays Essential for Variables

Lists

Python lists offer changeable and ordered data and written while accompanying square brackets, for example, "an apple," "cherry." Accessing an already existing list by referring to the index number while with the ability to write negative indexes such as '-1' or '-2'. You can also maneuver within your list and select a specific category of indexes by first determining your starting and endpoints. The return value with therefore be the range of specified items. You can also specify a scale of negative indexes, alter the value of the current item, loop between items on the list, add or remove items, and confirming if items are available.

Dictionaries

Python dictionaries comprise of indexed, changeable but unordered items typically written while with curly brackets with keys and values. Some of the activities involved include item access by use of a keyword inside the parentheses; conduct value changes, loop, check critical availability, length of the dictionary, and both adding and removing unwanted items. Besides, Python allows you to copy the dictionary by writing 'dict2 = dict1'. 'dict2' will become a representation to 'dict1' therefore makes any necessary changes automatically. Another way of creating a copy is also by using a built-in Dictionary technique, that is, 'copy.'

In other instances, Python dictionaries can also have other dictionaries within it a process referred to as nested dictionaries. You can readily determine the number of dictionaries present in the nest through creating of three already available. You can also generate your dictionary through the 'dict()' contractor function. The function enables the copying of the earlier dictionary or the creation of a completely new one. Within the Python dictionary, there exist several built-in techniques to implement and enjoy the efficiency of the dictionaries present.

Naming Variables

The naming of variables remains straightforward, and both beginners and experienced programmers can readily perform the process. However, providing titles to these variables accompany specific rules to ensure the provision of the right name. Consistency, style, and adhering to variable naming rules ensure that you create an excellent and reliable name to use both today and the future. The rules are:

- Names must have a single word, that is, with no spaces

- Names must only comprise of letters and numbers as well as underscores such as (_)

- The first letter must never be a number

- Reserved words must never be used as variable names

When naming variables, you should bear in mind that the system is case-sensitive, hence avoid creating the same names within a single program to prevent confusion. Another important component when naming is considering the style. It entails beginning the title with a lowercase letter while using underscores as spaces between your words or phrases used. Besides, the program customarily prevents starting the name with a capital letter. Begin with a lowercase letter and either mix or use them consistently.

When creating variable names, it may seem so straightforward and easy, but sometimes it may become verbose henceforth becoming a disaster to beginners. However, the challenge of creating sophisticated names is quite beneficial for learned as it prepares you for the following tutorials. Similarly, Python enables you to write your desired name of any length consisting of lower- and upper-case letters, numbers as well as underscores. Python also offers the addition of complete Unicode support essential for Unicode features in variables.

Specific rules are governing the procedure for naming variables; hence adhere to them to create an exceptional name to your variables. Create more readable names that have meaning to prevent instances of confusion to your members, especially programmers. A more descriptive name is much preferred compares to others. However, the technique of naming variables remains illegible as different programmers decide on how they are going to create their kind of names.

Methods of Creating a Multi-Name for Python Variables

- Pascal case: this method entails the first, second, and subsequent words in the name as capitalized to enhance readability, for example, ConcentrationOfWhiteSmoke.

- Camel case: the second and subsequent words of the name created remains capitalized, for example, the ConcentrationOfWhiteSmoke.

- Snake case: snake method of creating variable names entails separator of words using an underscore as mentioned earlier, for example, concentration_of_white_smoke.

Learning Python Strings, Numbers and Tuple

Python strings are part of Python variables and comprise of objects created from enclosing characters or values in double-quotes. For example, 'var = Hello World'. With Python not supporting character types in its functions, they are however treated as strings of one more characters as well as substrings. Within the Python program, there exist several string operators making it essential for variables to be named and stored in different formats. Some of the string operators commonly used in Python are [], [:], 'in', r/R, %, + and *.

There exist several methods of strings today. Some include replacing Python string () to return a copy of the earlier value in a variable, changing the string format, that is, upper and lower cases and using the 'join' function, especially for concatenating variables. Other methods include the reverse function and split strings using the command 'word.split'. What to note is that strings play an important role, especially in naming and storage of values despite Python strings being immutable.

Types of Data Variables

String

A text string is a type of data variable represented in either String data types or creating a string from a range of type char. The syntax for string data comprises multiple declarations including 'char Str1[15], 'char Str5[8] = "ardiono"; among others. As to declare a string effectively, add null character 'Str3', declare arrays of chars without utilizing in the form of 'Str1' and initialize a given array and leave space for a larger string such as Str6. Strings are usually displayed with doubles quotes despite the several versions of available to construct strings for varying data types.

Char

Char are data types primarily used in variables to store character values with literal values written in single quotes, unlike strings. The values are stores in numbers form, but the specific encoding remains visibly suitable for performing arithmetic. For instance, you can see that it is saved as 'A' +, but it has a value of 66 as the ASCII 'A' value represents 66. Char data types are usually 8 bits, essential for character storage. Characters with larger volumes are stored in bytes. The syntax for this type of variable is 'char var = val'; where 'var' indicates variable name while 'val' represents the value assigned to the variable.

Byte

A byte is a data type necessary for storing 8-bit unsigned numbers that are between 0 to 255 and with a syntax of 'byte var = val;.' Like Char data type, 'var' represents variable name while 'val' stands for the value to he assigned that variable. The difference between char and byte is that char stores smaller characters and with a low space volume while byte stores values which are larger.

Int

Another type of data type variable is the int, which stores 16-bit value yielding an array of between -32,768 and 32,767, which varies depending on the different programming platforms. Besides, int stores 2's complement math, which is negative numbers, henceforth providing the capability for the variable to store a wide range of values in one reserve. With Python, this type of data variable storage enables transparency in arithmetic operations in an intended manner.

Unsigned int

Unsigned int also referred to, as unsigned integers are data types for storing up to 2 bytes of values but do not include negative numbers. The numbers are all positive with a range of 0 to 65,535 with Duo stores of up to 4 bytes for 32-byte values, which range from 0 to 4,294,967,195. In comparison, unsigned integers comprise positive values and have a much higher bit. The syntax for unsigned int is 'unsigned int var = val;' while an example code being 'unsigned int ledPin = 13;'

Float

Float data types are values with point numbers, that is to say, a number with a decimal point. Floating numbers usually indicate or estimate analog or continuous numbers, as they possess a more advanced resolution compared to integers. The numbers stored may range from the highest of 7.5162306E+38 and the lowest of -3.2095174E+38. Floating-point numbers remain stored in the form of 32 bits taking about 4 bytes per information fed.

Unsigned Long

This is data types of variables with an extended size hence it stores values with larger storages compare to other data types. It stores up to 32 bits for 4 bytes and does not include negative numbers henceforth has a range of 0 to 4,294,967,295. The syntax for the unsigned long data type is 'unsigned long var = val;' essential for storing characters with much larger sizes.

Chapter 4 How to Install Python

Installing Python (Windows)

Here we introduce the installation and operation of Python under the Windows environment. Since there is no built-in Python environment in the Windows operating system, it needs to be installed independently. The installation package can be downloaded from Python's official website (www.Python.org). After opening the official website search for the navigation bar that has a "Downloads" button.

The website recommends a link by default because it can detect your operating system and recommend the latest version of Python 3.x, 3.6.5. After entering the download page of the corresponding version, there is a basic introduction to the environment you are trying to download. Several different versions are mainly aimed at different operating system platforms. You can choose different files to download according to whether your system is 32-bit or 64-bit.

In the new page that opens, we can find other versions, including the latest test version and the required version 3.4. If you want to install a 64-bit version of 3.6.5, click the framed link on the current page.

At the bottom of the newly opened page, we can find several other links. The file that starts with the Windows entity represents the 64-bit version of Windows, while the file that does not include 64 represents the 32-bit version.

The website shows a compressed installation package (Windows x86-64 Embedded ZipFile), an executable installation file, and a Web-based installation file (Windows x86-64). It is most convenient to download the executable installation package.

Note: 64-bit version cannot be installed on a 32-bit system, but a 32-bit version can be installed on a 32-bit system or 64-bit system.

Install Python

The Windows executable installation package is easier to install. Just like installing other Windows applications, we just need to select the appropriate option and click "Next" to complete the installation.

When the options appear in the installation, do not rush to the following step (the system demonstrated here is 64-bit in itself).

It must be noted that after "Add Python3.6 to PATH" is checked and Python 3.6 is added to the environment variable, Python's interactive prompt or Python's commands can be started directly and conveniently at the Windows command prompt in the future.

After selecting "Add Python 3.6 to PATH", select custom installation. Of course, it is also possible to select the first item for installation, which means Python is installed in the user directory of C disk. But at this time, you'd better know what the user directory is so that you can find the installed Python.exe files when necessary in the future.

Proceed with the instructions and python will be installed successfully in the system.

Installing Python (Mac)

If you're using a Mac, you can download the installation package from this link:

https://www.python.org/downloads/mac-osx/

The progression of learning is getting further into Python Programming Language. In reality, Python is an adaptable yet powerful language that can be used from multiple points of view. This just implies Python can be used intelligently when code or a declaration is to be tried on a line-by-line premise or when you're investigating its highlights. Incredibly, Python can be used in content mode, most notably, when you want to decipher a whole document of declarations or application program.

Working with Python, be that as it may, requires most extreme caution – mainly when you are drawing in or connecting with it. This caution is valid for each programming language as well. So as to draw in with Python intelligently, the Command Line window or the IDLE Development Environment can be used.

Since you are an apprentice of either programming by and large or using Python, there will shift ventures on how you could connect with and cooperate with Python programming language. The following are essential highlights of activities for brisk cooperation with Python:

The Command Line Interaction

Associating with the order line is the least demanding approach to work, as a novice, with Python. Python can simply be imagined by seeing how it functions through its reaction to each finished direction entered on the >>> brief. The Command Line probably won't be the most favored commitment with Python, at the same time, throughout the years, it has demonstrated to be the easiest method to investigate how Python functions for learners.

Launching Python using the Command Line

If you're using macOS, GNU/Linux, and UNIX frameworks, you should run the Terminal tool to get to the command line. Then again, if you are using Windows, you can get to the Python order line by right-clicking on the Start menu and launching Windows PowerShell.

As directions on programming require a contribution of an order, when you need Python to do something for you, you will train it by entering directions that it knows about a similar yield. This is an adjustment in the order may give the ideal yield; be cautious.

With this, Python will make an interpretation of these directions to guidelines that your PC or gadget can comprehend and execute.

Let's take a look at individual guides to perceive how Python functions. Note that you can use the print order to print the all-inclusive program

"Heydays, Savants!"

1. Above all else, open Python's command line.

2. At that point, at the >>>prompt, type the accompanying (don't leave space among print and the section): print ("Heydays, Savants!")

3. Now, you should press enter so as to disclose to Python that you're finished with the direction. Promptly, the direction line window will show Heydays, Savants! In the interim, Python has reacted similarly as it has been told in the composed arrangement that it can relate with. Then again, to perceive how it will react wrongly when you request that it print a similar string using a wrong linguistic structure for the print order, type and enter the accompanying direction on the Python order brief: Print("Heydays, Savants!")

The outcome will be: Syntax error: invalid language structure

This is a case of what get when you use invalid or fragmented explanations. Note that Python is a case-touchy programming language, so at whatever point you misunderstand the message it could be that you composed print with a capital letter. Obviously, there is a choice to print direction, you can simply type your announcement inside statements like this: "Primes, Savants!" Note that an announcement is the words you wish to show once the order is given; the words that can fit in are not confined to the model given here, however.

The most effective method to leave the Python order line

To exit from Python, you can type any of these commands: quit() or exit(). Subsequently, hold Control-Z and afterward press Enter; the Python should exit.

Your commonality with Python Programming ought to get fascinating now; there are still parts to learn, tolerance will satisfy.

The area of IDLE: Python's Integrated Development Environment (IDE)

A standout amongst the fascinating pieces of Python is the IDLE (Integrated Development and Learning Environment) apparatus. Despite the fact that this specific device is incorporated into Python's establishment bundle, you can download increasingly refined outsider IDEs as well. The IDLE instrument gives you access to an increasingly active stage to compose your code and work engagingly with Python. To get to IDLE, you can experience a similar organizer where you found the direction line symbol or on the begin menu (as you've gained from order line collaboration). When you click on the IDLE symbol, you will be coordinated to the Python Shell window. This will take us to the segment on cooperation with the Python Shell Window.

Connecting with the Python Shell Window

When you're at the Python Shell Window, you will see a dropdown menu and a >>>prompt that resembles what you've found in the direction line window (the primary connection talked about). There is a specific IDLE's function of altering for the drawing in past order.

Now, you will use a similar IDLE's altering menu to look back to your past directions, cut, copy, and glue past statements and, taking all things together, make any type of editing. Clearly the IDLE is increasingly similar to a jump from the direction line association. Incredibly, in the menu dropdown of the Python Shell window are the accompanying menu things: File, Windows, Help, Shell, Options, Edit, and Debug. Every one of these menus has various functions. The Shell and Debug menus are used while making more significant projects as they give get highlights to the procedure. In any case, while the Shell menu gives you a chance to restart the shell or look the shell's log for latest reset, Debug Menu has loads of valuable things for following the source record of an exemption and featuring the blundering line. With the Debugger option, you will most likely introduce an intelligent debugger window that will enable you to step and look through the running projects on the Python. The Options menu of the window enables you to edit and set IDLE to suit your own Python working inclinations.

Start Python

Python can be started in two ways.

1) Start Python's Own IDLE

If you want to run Python, you can click the "start" button on the Windows desktop and enter "IDLE" in the search box that appears to launch a Python desktop application to provide a prompt of "read-evaluate-print-loop quickly".

IDLE is Python's own simple IDE (Integrated Development Environment), which is Python's graphical interface editor. IDLE can be regarded as a simple version of an integrated development environment. Its function looks simple, but it is helpful for beginners to learn the Python language itself.

Here, a REPL environment is provided, that is, it reads the user's input ("Read"), returns to the car, evaluates and calculates ("Evaluate"), then prints the result ("Print"), and then a prompt "Loop" appears, thus circulating.

2) Start Python at Windows Prompt

Another way to start Python is to run Python programs through the Windows command prompt, and enter "cmd" in the Windows search box (or press "Win+R" key to open the run prompt box, note the "Win" key on the keyboard), or click the start button to enter "cmd" in the pop-up search box and enter to start the Windows command line window.

Note: the flashing cursor after ">" seen here is the command prompt provided by Windows.

When installing Python, since the "Add Python 3.6 to PATH" option is checked and the installed Python is added to the environment variable of Windows, Python can be successfully started by entering "python" after the prompt ">".

The prompt "> > >" indicates that Python installation was successful and Python has been started. The prompt "> > >" is Python-specific.

Next, "print("Hello Python!" is executed in either the first or second startup mode.) ".

If you want to return to the Windows command prompt, you can reach the goal by pressing the shortcut key "Ctrl+Z".

The above two methods are both REPL forms, suitable for writing relatively short programs or commands, and have the advantages of simplicity and flexibility. If the program has more functions and more modules or packages are called, the REPL form is not very convenient to maintain.

Chapter 5 Designing and Using Functions

Python Functions

Python functions are a right way of organizing the structure of our code. The functions can be used for grouping sections of code that are related. The work of functions in any programming language is to improve the modularity of code and make it possible to reuse code.

Python comes with many in-built functions. An excellent example of such a function is the "print()" function which we use for displaying the contents on the screen. Despite this, we can create our functions in Python. Such functions are referred to as the "user-defined functions".

To define a function, we use the "def" keyword which is then followed by the name of the function, and then the parenthesis (()).

The parameters or the input arguments have to be placed inside the parenthesis. The parameters can also be defined within parenthesis. The function has a body or the code block and this must begin with a colon (:) and it has to be indented. It is suitable for you to note that the default setting is that the arguments have a positional behavior. This means that they should be passed while following the order in which you defined them.

Example:

```
#!/usr/bin/python3

def functionExample():

    print('The function code to run')

    bz = 10 + 23

    print(bz)
```

We have defined a function named functionExample. The parameters of a function are like the variables for the function. The parameters are usually added inside the parenthesis, but our above function has no parameters. When you run above code, nothing will happen since we simply defined the function and specified what it should do. The function can be called as shown below:

```
#!/usr/bin/python3

def functionExample():

    print('The function code to run')

    bz = 10 + 23

functionExample()
```

It will print this:

```
The function code to run
```

That is how we can have a basic Python function.

Function Parameters

You can dynamically define arguments for a function. Example:

```python
#!/usr/bin/python3

def additionFunction(n1,n2):

    result = n1 + n2

    print('The first number is', n1)

    print('The second number is', n2)

    print("The sum is", result)

additionFunction(10,5)
```

The code returns the following result:

```
The first number is 10
The second number is 5
The sum is 15
```

We defined a function named addFunction. The function takes two parameters namely n1 and n2. We have another variable named result which is the sum of the two function parameters. In the last statement, we have called the function and passed the values for the two parameters. The function will calculate the value of variable result by adding the two numbers. We finally get the result shown above.

Note that during our function definition, we specified two parameters, n1 and n2. Try to call the function will either more than two parameters, or 1 parameter and see what happens. Example:

```
#!/usr/bin/python3

def additionFunction(n1,n2):

    result = n1 + n2

    print('The first number is', n1)

    print('The second number is', n2)

    print("The sum is", result)

additionFunction(5)
```

In the last statement in our code above, we have passed only one argument to the function, that is, 5. The program gives an error when executed:

```
Traceback (most recent call last):
  File "main.py", line 9, in
    additionFunction(5)
TypeError: additionFunction() missing 1 required positional argument: 'n2'
```

The error message simply tells us one argument is missing. What if we run it with more than two arguments?

```
#!/usr/bin/python3

def additionFunction(n1,n2):

    result = n1 + n2
```

print('The first number is', n1)

print('The second number is', n2)

print("The sum is", result)

additionFunction(5,10,9)

We also get an error message:

```
Traceback (most recent call last):
  File "main.py", line 9, in
    additionFunction(5,10,9)
TypeError: additionFunction() takes 2 positional arguments but 3 were given
```

The error message tells us the function expects two arguments but we have passed 3 to it.

In most programming languages, parameters to a function can be passed either by reference or by value. Python supports parameter passing only by reference. This means if what the parameter refers to is changed in the function; the same change will also be reflected in the calling function. Example:

#!/usr/bin/python3

def referenceFunction(ls1):

print ("List values before change: ", ls1)

ls1[0]=800

print ("List values after change: ", ls1)

return

Calling the function

ls1 = [940,1209,6734]

referenceFunction(ls1)

print ("Values outside function: ", ls1)

The code gives this result:

```
List values before change:  [940, 1209, 6734]
List values after change:   [800, 1209, 6734]
Values outside function:    [800, 1209, 6734]
```

What we have done in this example is that we have maintained the reference of the objects which are being passed and then values have been appended to the same function.

In following example below, we are passing by reference then the same reference will be overwritten inside the same function which has been called:

#!/usr/bin/python3

def referenceFunction(ls1):

  ls1 = [11,21,31,41]

  print ("Values inside the function: ", ls1)

  return

ls1 = [51,91,81]

referenceFunction(ls1)

print ("Values outside function: ", ls1)

The code gives this result:

```
Values inside the function:  [11, 21, 31, 41]
Vlaues outside function:  [51, 91, 81]
```

Note that the "ls1" parameter will be local to the function "referenceFunction". Even if this is changed within the function, the "ls1" will not be affected in any way. As the output shows above, the function helps us achieve nothing.

Function Parameter Defaults

There are default parameters for functions, which the function creator can use in his or her functions. This means that one has the choice of using the default parameters, or even using the ones they need to use by specifying them. To use the default parameters, the parameters having defaults are expected to be last ones written in function parameters. Example:

#!/usr/bin/python3

def myFunction(n1, n2=6):

   pass

In above example, the parameter n2 has been given a default value unlike parameter n1. The parameter n2 has been written as the last one in the function parameters. The values for such a function may be accessed as follows:

```
#!/usr/bin/python3

def windowFunction(width,height,font='TNR'):

    # printing everything

    print(width,height,font)

windowFunction(245,278)
```

The code outputs the following:

245 278 TNR

The parameter font had been given a default value, that is, TNR. In the last line of the above code, we have passed only two parameters to the function, that is, the values for width and height parameters. However, after calling the function, it returned the values for the three parameters. This means for a parameter with default, we don't need to specify its value or even mention it when calling the function.

However, it's still possible for you to specify the value for the parameter during function call. You can specify a different value to what had been specified as the default and you will get the new one as value of the parameter. Example:

```
#!/usr/bin/python3

def windowFunction(width,height,font='TNR'):

    # printing everything
```

```
print(width,height,font)
```

```
windowFunction(245,278,'GEO')
```

The program outputs this:

```
245  278  GEO
```

Above, the value for parameter was given the default value "TNR". When calling the function in the last line of the code, we specified a different value for this parameter, which is "GEO". The code returned the value as "GEO". The default value was overridden.

Chapter 6 A Modular Approach to Program Organization

M odules, also known as packages, are a set of names. This is usually a library of functions and object classes that are made available to be used within different programs. We used the notion of modules earlier in this part to use some function from the math library. We are going to cover in-depth on how to develop and define modules. To use modules in a Python program, the following statements are used: import, from, reload. The first one imports the whole module. The second allows import only a specific name or element from the module. The third one, reload, allows reloading a code of a module while Python is running and without stopping in it. Before digging into their definition and development, let's start first by the utility of modules or packages within Python.

Modules Concept and Utility within Python

Modules are a very simple way to make a system component organized. Modules allow reusing the same code over and over. So far, we were working in a Python interactive session. Every code we have written and tested is lost once we exit the interactive session. Modules are saved in files that make them persistent, reusable, and sharable. You can consider modules as a set of files where you can define functions, names, data objects, attributes, and so on. Modules are a tool to group several components of a system in a single place. In Python programming, modules are among the highest-level unit. They point to the name of packages and tools. Besides, they allow the sharing of the implemented data. You only need one copy of the module to be able to use across a large program. If an object is to be used in different functions and programs, coding it as a module allows share it with other programmers.

To have a sense of the architecture of Python coding, we go through some general structure explanation. We have been using so far in this very simple code examples that do not have high-level structure. In large applications, a program is a set of several Python files. By Python files, we mean files that contain Python code and have a .py extension. There is one main high-level program and the other files are the modules. The high-level file consists of the main code that dictates the control flow and executes the application. Module files define the tools that are needed to process elements and components of the main program and maybe elsewhere. The main program makes use of the tools that are specified in the modules.

In their turn, modules make use of tools that are specified in other modules. When you import a module in Python, you have access to every tool that is declared or defined in that specific module. Attributes are the variables or the functions associated with the tools within a module. Hence, when a module is imported, we have access to the attributes of the tools as well to process them. For instance, let's consider we have two Python files named file1.py and file2.py where the file1.py is the main program and file2.py is the module. In the file2.py, we have a code that defines the following function:

```
def Xfactorial (X):
```

```
P = 1
```

```
for i in range (1, X + 1):
```

```
P *= i
```

```
return P
```

To use this function in the main program, we should define code statements in the file1.py as follows:

```
Import file2
```

```
A = file2.Xfactorial (3)
```

The first line imports the module file2.py. This statement means to load the file file2.py. This gives access to the file1.py to all tools and functions defined in file2.py by the name file2. The function Xfactorial is called by the second line. The module file2.py is where this function is defined using the attributes' syntax. The line file2.Xfactorial() means fetch any name value of Xfactorial and lies within the code body of file2. In this example, it is a function that is callable. So, we have provided an input argument and assigned the output result to the variable A. If we add a third statement to print the variable A and run the file file1.py, it would display 6 which is the factorial of 3. Along Python, you will see the attribute syntax as object.attribute. This allows calling the attributes that might be a function or data object that provides properties of the object.

Note that some modules that you might import when programming with Python are available in Python itself. As we have mentioned at the beginning of this book, Python comes with a standard large library that has built-in modules. These modules support all common tasks that might be needed in programming from operating system interfaces to graphical user interface. They are not part of the language. However, they can be imported and comes with a software installation package. You can check the complete list of available modules in a manual that comes with the installation or goes to the official Python website: www.Python.org. This manual is kept updated every time a new version of Python is released.

How to Import a Module

We have talked about importing a module without really explaining what happens behind in Python. Imports are a very fundamental concept in Python programming structure. In this section, we are going to cover in-depth how really Python imports modules within a program. Python follows three steps to import a file or a module within the work environment of a program. The first step consists of finding the file that contains the module. The second step consists of compiling the module to a byte-code if required. Finally, the third step runs the code within the module file to build the objects that are defined. These three steps are run only when the module is imported for the first time during the execution of a program. This module and all its objects are loaded in the memory. When the module is imported further in the program, it skips all three steps and just fetch the objects defined by the module and are saved in memory.

At the very first step of importing a module, Python has to find the module file location. Note that, so far in the examples we presented, we used import without providing the complete path of the module or extension .py. We just used import math, or import file2.py (an example of the earlier section). Python import statement omits the extension and the path. We just simply import a module by its name. The reason for this is that Python has a module that looks for paths called 'search path module'. This module is used specifically to find the path of module files that are imported by the import statements.

In some cases, you might need to configure the path search of modules to be able to use new modules that are not part of the standard library. You need to customize it to include these new modules. The search path is simply the concatenation of the home directory, directories of PYTHONPATH, directories of the standard library, and optionally if the content of files with extension .pth when they exist. The home directory is set automatically by the system to a directory of Python executable when launched from the interactive session, or it can be modified to the working directory where your program is saved. This directory is the first to be searched when import a module is run without a path. Hence, if your home directory points to a directory that includes your program along with the modules, importing these modules does not require any path specification.

The directory of the standard library is also searched automatically. This directory contains all default libraries that come with Python. The directories of PYTHONPATH can be set to point toward the directory of new modules that are developed. In fact, PTYHONPATH is an environment variable that contains a list of directories that contains Python files. When PTYHONPATH is set, all these paths are included in the Python environment and the search path directory would search these directories too when importing modules. Python also allows defining a file with .pth extension that contains directories, one in each line. This file serves the same as PTYHONPATH when included appropriately in a directory. You can check the directories' paths included when you run Python using sys.path. You simply print sys.path to get the list of the directories that Python will be searching for.

Remember, when importing a module, we just use the name of the module without its extension. When Python is searching for a module in its environment paths, it selects the first name that matches the module name regardless of the extension. Because Python allows using packages that are coded in other languages, it does not simply select a module with .py extension but a file name or even a zip file name that matches the module name being imported. Therefore, you should name your modules distinctly and configure the search path in a manner that makes it obvious to choose a module.

When Python finds the source code of the module file with a name that corresponds to the name in the import statement, it will compile it into byte code in case it is required. This step is skipped if Python finds an already byte code file with no source code. If the source code has been modified, another byte code file is automatically regenerated by Python while the program runs in other further executions. Byte code files have typically .pyc extension. When Python is searching and finds the module file name, it will load the byte code file that corresponds to the latest version of the source code with .py extension. If the source code is newer than the byte code file, it will generate a new one by compiling the source code file. Note that only imported files have corresponding files with .pyc extension. These files, the byte code files, are stored on your machine to make the imports faster in future use.

The third step of the import statement is running the module's byte code. Each statement and each assignment in the file are executed. This allows generating any function, data objects, and so on defined in the module. The functions and all attributes are accessed within the program via importers. During this step, you will see print statements if they exist. The 'def ' statement will create a function object to be used in the main program.

To summarize the import statement, it involves searching for the file, compiling it, and running the byte code file. All other import statements use the module stored in memory and ignore all the three steps. When first imported, Python will look in the search path module to select the module. Hence, it is important to configure correctly the path environment variable to point to the directory that contains new defined modules. Now that you have the big picture and the concept of modules, let's explore how we can define and develop new modules.

Chapter 7 Using Methods

S tring literals are usually surrounded by single quotation marks and double quotation marks. For example, the world expression 'string' is written in the same way as "string." You can print it in the shell with the print() function, just like I did with the data types in Python shell. The first step is to assign a string to some variable of your choice. You can write down the name of the variable that you want to use, which can be followed by the equal sign and then the string. Please note that you can use either a single alphabet or a full name as the name of a variable. Use them wisely in a program so that when you read the code, you know the job of each variable.

>>> myString = "I am learning deep learning with python."

>>> print(myString)

I am learning deep learning with python.

>>> myString = "I am studying deep learning with python."

>>> print(myString)

I am studying deep learning with python.

>>> myString = """I am studying deep learning,

with Python,

and I am really enjoying it,

and writing programs with it."""

```
>>> print(myString)
```

I am studying deep learning,

with Python,

and I am really enjoying it,

and writing programs with it.

```
>>> myString = "'I am studying deep learning,
```

with Python,

and I am really enjoying it,

and writing programs with it.'"

```
>>> print(myString)
```

I am studying deep learning,

with Python,

and I am really enjoying it,

and writing programs with it.

```
>>>
```

Like many programming languages, Python strings are like byte arrays, which represent Unicode characters. There is no character data type in Python. However, a single character is a string that has a length of 1. You can use square brackets to access elements of the string.

```
>>> myString = """I am studying deep learning,

with Python,

and I am really enjoying it,

and writing programs with it."""
>>> print(myString[10])

i

>>> print(myString[1])

>>> print(myString[2])

a

>>> print(myString[0])

I

>>>
```

Do you love slicing? Slicing always has a satisfying effect on the human brain. Python strings offer you the freedom to return a wide range of characters with the help of using the slice syntax. The first step in this regard is to specify the starting index and the ending index. Separate the two by a colon to return a part of the string.

```
>>> myString = """I am studying deep learning,

with Python,

and I am really enjoying it,
```

and writing programs with it."""

```
>>> print(myString[20:35])
```

earning,

with P

```
>>> print(myString[10:35])
```

ing deep learning,

with P

```
>>> print(myString[0:50])
```

I am studying deep learning,

with Python,

and I am

```
>>>
```

Python allows you to slice a string by using negative indexing as well. Let's see how you can do that. The only difference is that you will use negative numbers in the string.

```
>>> myString = """I am studying deep learning,
```

with Python,

and I am really enjoying it,

and writing programs with it."""

```
>>> print(myString[-50:-1])
```

really enjoying it,

and writing programs with it

```
>>> print(myString[-60:-1])
```

,

and I am really enjoying it,

and writing programs with it

```
>>> print(myString[-70:-10])
```

ith Python,

and I am really enjoying it,

and writing program

```
>>>
```

You can calculate the total length of a string by using the following code.

```
>>> myString = """I am studying deep learning,
```

with Python,

and I am really enjoying it,

and writing programs with it."""

```
>>> print(len(myString))
```

100

>>>

String Methods

The first method that will come under discussion is the strip() method that does the job of removing whitespaces from your string at the start or the end.

>>> myString = """ I am studying deep learning,

with Python,

and I am really enjoying it,

and writing programs with it. """

>>> print(myString.strip())

I am studying deep learning,

with Python,

and I am really enjoying it,

and writing programs with it.

>>>

In the following example, I will try three different methods on the same string. One method is to convert the text into a lower case; the second is to convert it into the upper case, while the third is to convert the text into title case. All of them are simple and very handy when you are composing messages that you have to display for your users.

>>> myString = """I am studying deep learning,

with Python,

and I am really enjoying it,

and writing programs with it."""

```
>>> print(myString.lower())
```

i am studying deep learning,

with python,

and i am really enjoying it,

and writing programs with it.

```
>>> print(myString.upper())
```

I AM STUDYING DEEP LEARNING,

WITH PYTHON,

AND I AM REALLY ENJOYING IT,

AND WRITING PROGRAMS WITH IT.

```
>>> print(myString.title())
```

I Am Studying Deep Learning,

With Python,

And I Am Really Enjoying It,

And Writing Programs with It.

```
>>>
```

Let's talk about some more string methods to learn how it operates.

```
>>> myString = """I am studying deep learning,

with Python,

and I am really enjoying it,

and writing programs with it."""
>>> print(myString.replace("studying", "reading"))
I am reading deep learning,

with Python,

and I am really enjoying it,

and writing programs with it.
>>> print(myString.replace("really", " "))
I am studying deep learning,

with Python,

and I am   enjoying it,

and writing programs with it.
>>> print(myString.replace("really", ""))
I am studying deep learning,

with Python,

and I am  enjoying it,
```

and writing programs with it.

```
>>> print(myString.replace("studying",""))
```

I am deep learning,

with Python,

and I am really enjoying it,

and writing programs with it.

```
>>>
```

In the above example, I attempted to replace a word with a new word. Then I moved on to eliminating a word by replacing it with no word. I tried it thrice to explain how you can manage extra whitespaces that are likely to happen if you don't fix them. The best method is to eliminate extra spaces from the code. There is a special method known as the split() method that can split the string into several substrings.

```
>>> myString = """I am studying deep learning,
```

with Python,

and I am really enjoying it,

and writing programs with it."""

```
>>> print(myString.split(","))
```

['I am studying deep learning,' '\nwith Python,' '\nand I am really enjoying it,' '\nand writing programs with it.']

```
>>> myString = "I, am, studying, deep, learning."
```

```
>>> print(myString.split(","))
```

`['I', ' am', ' studying', ' deep', ' learning.']`

```
>>>
```

There is another interesting method using which you can check if a certain phrase or a character exists in a particular string or not. There are two keywords 'in' or 'not in' that you can use for this method.

```
>>> myString = "I am studying deep learning."
```

```
>>> a = "studying" not in myString
```

```
>>> print(a)
```

False

```
>>> a = "studying" in myString
```

```
>>> print(a)
```

True

```
>>>
```

If you can recall the data types that I have shared with you earlier on, you will realize that Python is communicating with you in the Boolean data type. You have got the answer in False and True to your query. This method is the way to extract more information about a Python string through a specific method.

If you have got two strings, you can combine them easily by using the Python string concatenation method. The primary operator that you can use here is the '+' operator. Let's see how to do that.

```
>>> myString = "I am studying deep learning."

>>> myString1 = "with Python."

>>> combstring = myString + myString1

>>> print(combstring)

I am studying deep learning with Python.

>>> myString = "I am studying deep learning."

>>> myString1 = " with Python."

>>> combstring = myString + myString1

>>> print(combstring)

I am studying deep learning with Python.

>>>
```

The above code snippet has two similar code examples. The first one has a flaw. There is no whitespace in the first after the word learning. Two words have been wrongly combined. I fixed the issue by adding whitespace at the start of the second string. This formula will be helpful for you when you are combining two strings for writing a program. This method is the easiest; however, there is another method that you can use to add necessary space between two strings. Both play the same role, so it is up to you which one you like the most.

```
>>> myString = "I am studying deep learning."

>>> myString1 = "with Python."

>>> combString = myString + " " + myString1

>>> print(combString)

I am studying deep learning with Python.

>>>
```

You can format your string at will by the following method. Formatting a string means that you can combine two data types when you are writing a program for a user. If you try to concatenate them by using the same technique that we used for two strings, this is unlikely to work for you. Let's see what happens when you try to do that.

```
>>> myString = 23

>>> myString1 = "I am John and I am " + myString

Traceback (most recent call last):

  File "<pyshell#98>", line 1, in <module>

    myString1 = "I am John and I am " + myString

TypeError: can only concatenate str (not "int") to str
```

Don't worry. There is a special method for this purpose, the format() method. This method picks up the passed arguments, formats them, and then adds them to the string where you put in the placeholders {}. Let's see how to insert numbers.

>>> myString = 23

>>> myString1 = "I am John and I am {}"

>>> print(myString1.format(myString))

I am John and I am 23

Chapter 8 Processing Files in Python

In Python, files are considered as a data object. In fact, Python has a built-in data object type assigned specifically for files, the file data object is associated only with common methods used to process files. The built-in method open is a function that allows creating a file data object to be processed. In short, this method links the file data object to the file stored in the hardware of your machine. Once you call open function, you have access to the file in order to read it or write it using the read and write attributes of the file data object.

The table presented below lists all common methods used to process files. In order to read a file, the function open is called with file name along with the mode to process the file which is 'r' in this case. To write a file, the process mode is 'w'. This mode creates a new file. If a file exists with the same name used to open a file in a writing mode, it will be overwritten. In order to write or add content into the existing file, the file should be open with mode append (i.e. 'a').

The file name can include or not the file path of the directory that contains or will contain the file. If the path is not specified, then Python would assume that the file is in the working directory which is the directory where the current program is running.

List of Methods to Process File

Method	Explanation
File2Read = open (file_path/file_name, 'r')	Defines a file data object to write
File2write = open (file_path/file_name, 'w')	Defines a file data object to read
content = File2read.read()	Reads the whole file and assign the content to a single string
content = File2read.read(X)	Reads only X bytes
Line = File2read.readLine()	Reads following line
Lines = File2read.readLins()	Reads the whole file and stores the content in a line strings list
File2write(data)	Writes data in the file
File2write.writeLine(List_line)	Writes in the file the strings line of the list List_line
File2write.close()	Closes the file manually

After you open a file, you have a file data object. Then, its methods can be used in reading and writing with the methods presented in the table above. In either case, the file data object methods take and return only strings in Python. In other words, the read method returns as a data object type as a string. The write method takes as data object type as string, too. Both methods have different varieties.

The role of the close method is closing the connection between Python and the external file residing in the hardware of your machine. Python also liberates the space in memory that was occupied by an object after it is no longer referenced in the script. Python would also close automatically the close if required. Hence, in Python, it is not necessary to call the close method in order to delete the file object reference manually. However, it is good practice to call the close method after you finish reading or writing a file.

Example File Processing in Python

In this section, we are going to present some examples of processing files in Python using the methods presented in Table 10. The first example illustrates how to write the 'Hello World' in a file. So, let's go back to prompt shell and launch Python for practice.

```
>>> File = open (' MyFile.txt', 'w')
>>> File.write(' Hello World! \n')
>>> File.close()
```

In the first statement, we called the method open in write mode (i.e. 'w') to create the file. The second statement writes the line 'Hello World!' with a newline marker. The third statement closes the file object. In the following code example, we are going to open the file in reading mode (i.e. 'r') and get the line written in the file:

```
>>> File = open (' MyFile.txt', 'r')

>>> A = File.readline()

>>> print (' This is an example of reading a file with readline: \n', A)

This is an example of reading a file with readline:

 Hello World!

>>> File.close()
```

Now, we are going to add a second line in our file. To do so, we are going to open the file in mode append (i.e. 'a') and write the line 'My first file in Python':

```
>>> File = open (' MyFile.txt', 'a')

>>> File.write(' This is my first file in Python')

>>> File.close()
```

If we open the file again and check its content with the read method, we get the following output:

```
>>> File = open (' MyFile.txt', 'r')

>>> A = File.read()
```

>>> print (' This is an example of reading a file with read: \n',

A)

This is an example of reading a file with read:

Hello World!

This is my first file in Python

>>> File.close()

As you can notice when opening a file with append mode, it adds whatever you write in the file at the end. We can also change what is already in the file by opening the file in mode 'r+'. When you open the file in this mode and write in it, it will overwrite everything in it. For instance:

>>> File = open (' MyFile.txt', 'r+')

>>> File.write(' This is my first file Python opened in mode

r+')

>>> File.close()

>>> File = open (' MyFile.txt', 'r')

>>> A = File.read()

>>> print (' Checking file after opening in mode r+: \n', A)

Checking file after opening in mode r+:

This is my first file Python opened in mode r+

>>>File.close()

Remember, loops are very handy when it comes to repeating the same tasks for a specific number of times. In particular, loops are very useful in processing the file data object. We have seen through the above examples that we can read the content of the whole file in one single step using the read method. In some cases, we need to read the file line by line. In this case, we would use the readLine method. We might also need to write the file line by line in the case of formatted files, in which case, the writelines is handy. Let's practice some examples. First, we are going to write using writelines method. Then we are going to read the same file line by line. For both tasks, we will use a while loop.

```
>>> List_string = [' This is an example of \n',

... 'writing a file \n',

... ' on multiple lines\n',

... ' using write Lines \n',

... ' inside a while loop']

>>>print (' List of strings is:\n ', List_string)
```

List of strings is:

[' This is an example of \n', 'writing a file \n', ' on multiple lines\n', ' using write Lines', ' inside a while loop']

```
>>> File = open ('Test', 'w')

>>> File.writelines (List_string)

>>> File.close ()
```

Remember that all file object methods process only strings. Therefore, we created a list of strings where each element end with /n for newline maker. Now, we open the file for reading:

>>> File = open ('Test', 'r')

>>> while 1:

... Line = File.readline ()

... if not Line: break

... print (Line)

...

This is an example of

writing a file

on multiple lines

using write Lines inside a while loop

>>> File.close ()

As you can notice, we have a break statement in the while loop. This ensures that the while loop stops when there is no line to read. In other words, it ensures that the loop exit when it reaches the end of the file. Because 1 is always evaluated to true, the loop will continue running until it runs to the break. Hence, this loop reads the file line by line until it reaches the end of the file. If we open the file and use the read method, we get exactly the same results:

```
>>> File = open ('Test', 'r')

>>> A = File.read ()
```

>>> print ('This is the output from reading the file with reading method: \n', A)

This is the output from reading the file with reading method:

This is an example of

writing a file

on multiple lines

using write Lines inside a while loop

```
>>> File.close ()
```

Note in this last example, we did not specify the file extension. In fact, Python allows handling and processing any type of files that the extension does not matter. These methods work the same on any file.

Chapter 9 Python Algorithms

Some of the Best Python Algorithms for Data Analysis

We have spent some time in this guide looking at some of the basics of the Python language, as well as some of the basics of data analysis and what we are able to do with this for some of our own needs. Now it is time for us to take both of these ideas and put them together.

In order to complete a good data analysis in the first place, we need to be able to run the data that we have collected through a number of algorithms, usually, a few, though in some cases, one will be fine. These algorithms are going to help us to learn what patterns and insights are found in that data, and can give us some good predictions in the end.

There are a number of different Python data analysis algorithms that we are able to work with along the way, and it is going to often depend on the what we would like to do with that data to start with, and how we are able to benefit from this as well. With this in mind, let's dive right into some of the basics that come with these algorithms, and learn a bit more about why Python algorithms are the best for data analysis.

Neural Networks

The first kind of Python algorithm that we are able to use for data analysis is going to be known as the neural network. This is a fairly sophisticated type of algorithm to work with in the first place, but it is going to provide you with a lot of the power and more that you need to get some of the work done.

The neural network is going to work in a manner similar to how the brain will function. It is going to form connections to the things that it gets right, and it can remember this for future use as well. This helps it to learn as time goes on, and makes it easier and faster and more efficient at some of the work that it needs to complete as well. Once it has been able to go through and learn something new, you will find that it will remember it in the future.

In addition, the neural network is really good at helping with things like identifying what is in an image. It does this by going through the different layers of the pictures, one at a time, and then making a good prediction of what is going to be found in that image. The more layers that it is able to go through, the more accurate it will be at guessing what is in the picture as well. This makes it an effective tool to use for many of the projects you are working with.

However, we have to keep in mind that the computational costs are going to be a bit higher with this one. Because we are working with an algorithm that is able to methodically go through a bunch of layers and make accurate predictions, we can see why the costs will be higher with this one. You have to determine ahead of time if this is the right kind of process for you to work with, or if one of the other algorithms out there would work better.

Clustering

There are a number of different clustering techniques that you are able to work with when it comes to handling a data analysis. These are all going to take the data, though and put them together in clusters so you can see more about the distribution of where your points of data are going to fall. There are different ways that you are able to work with clustering, and different ways that you can cluster up your data, but it is a good way to put the information into groups and see some good insights right away.

The number of clusters that you will have in your work is going to depend on what you are focusing on. For example, if you are working to divide your group into males and females, then you will only need to have two clusters. But if you would like to divide things up by the age of your customers, or by where they live in the country or the world, then you will probably need to have more than two clusters in order to have the best idea of what is going on.

With these clusters, you will be able to plot them on something like a scatterplot, and then figure out where everything is going to fall. This is a great way to figure out the best options to take, whether there is a new demographic that you need to work with, and more. You can just put these clusters on your scatterplot, and you can learn a lot of information in a short amount of time.

The idea of these clusters is pretty simple. When you have some data points that fall into the same cluster, you can safely make the assumption that the points are going to have some similarities with one another. But if the data points are not in the same cluster, then this is a sign that they are going to be different from one another. If we are able to keep this in mind, it is a lot easier for us to work with understanding this kind of algorithm.

Support Vector Machines

These are going to be the algorithms that you are able to use in order to figure out the right course of action to take. When you see that the line and the hyperplane come together, then this is a good idea that the information that is there is going to lead you to the results that you are looking for. This can make picking out the right decision easier, as long as you know the right steps that are going to help you to get the best results as well.

The biggest trick that comes with this one sometimes is figuring out which lines and hyperplanes we should pick and work with. Sometimes, depending on the type of data that you are working with and what is all in it, you will end up with more than one hyperplane. Sometimes this will not be a big deal because you will be able to see which one is the best for your needs. Other times it may seem like there is more than one answer that is going to work the best for your needs as well.

There are a number of options that we are able to work in order to pick out the right SVM for what we want to do. You will learn how to do this more with experience, but you will be able to learn about your data and then figure this out as well. Sometimes experimenting with a few of these to see which one is the best is another good option that we are able to choose as well.

Naïve Bayes

The Naïve Bayes algorithm is a good choice to go with when you want to do a bit of exploration with the data in the beginning. Maybe you want to see what the best way is to split up the data that you have, or you are not yet certain about what kind of algorithm is going to be the best one for you to focus your attention on yet. In some cases, you may need to show some of the data and some of the information that you have ahead of time, right after collecting it, to those who want to see what is going on, but may not understand all of the more technical aspects that come with it.

This is where the Naïve Bayes algorithm is going to come into play and can really help us. With this option, we are able to take a good exploration of the data that we have, and then determine the best steps to take after. Sometimes this helps us to choose which of the other algorithms are the best ones for us to go with. And other times, it may be a good way to create a beginner's model so that we can show this off before being able to finish all of the work for the final project.

The Naïve Bayes algorithm is usually not going to be the first choice that we make when it is time to handle some of our data, and we will usually go through and make a few other adjustments to the process as well and finish off with another kind of algorithm. But it is definitely a good algorithm to go with because it adds in a lot of the different parts that you need to get a good idea about what the data contains, and what else we are able to do with it along the way.

Decision Trees

Another option that we are able to go with here is the decision trees. These trees are going to help us to make some good decisions and compare some of the likely outcomes of the decisions that we do make. If you are uncertain about which steps to take, especially if you have a few choices to pick from, then the decision tree is going to be one of the best algorithms for you to choose from.

To start, you would be able to ask your question and implement it in the information or the data that you have. Of course, we first need to clean and organize it, but we will assume that this part is already done. When you are ready, the data can tell us which steps are the best, and the likely outcome of each choice that you try to make along the way. This can help you to make some better decisions because you can look at the data in a more clear and organized manner, and you know that it actually makes sound sense, rather than just using your intuition along the way.

In addition, you are able to take a bunch of these decision trees and combine them together into a random forest. The random forest is simply going to be when we combine together a bunch of those decision trees in order to compare more than one option.

Maybe you want to see which is best for you. If you ever want to compare more than one idea or thought for you to take, and then working with the random forest, or even a simple decision tree, can get this done. You just add in the information that you want to work with, and then compare the decisions and their potential outcomes before going.

As we can see, there are a lot of different types of algorithms that we are able to use when it comes to handling our data and making sure that it makes as much sense as possible. A bit point of working with data analysis is to help us to sort through all of that data. Otherwise, that data is just going to sit around and be worthless to us and just sitting there taking up space.

Each of the algorithms that we went through above is meant to help us to figure out different ways that we are able to move around our data, and different ways that we will come to a better understanding of what is inside of our data, and how we can use that.

Whether you want to be able to make smarter decisions for your business, or you are looking for ways to find new customers or beat out the competition, the algorithms above, with the help of the Python code, will be able to help you get there.

Chapter 10 Databases

D ata management is not a scientific discipline per se. However, increasingly, it permeates the activities of basic scientific work. The increasing volume of data and increasing complexity has long exceeded manageability through simple spreadsheets.

Currently, the need to store quantitative, qualitative data and media of different formats (images, videos, sounds) is very common in an integrated platform from which they can be easily accessed for analysis, visualization or simply consultation.

The Python language has simple solutions to solve this need at its most different levels of sophistication. Following the Python included batteries, its standard library introduces us to the Pickle and cPickle module and, starting with Version 2.5, the SQLite3 relational database.

Specifying the Database

johnsmith= os.path.expanduser (' ~ /. johnsmith')

if not os.path.exists (at the dir):

os.mkdir (at the dir)

sqlhub.process Connection = connectionForURI (' sqlite://'+johnsmithr +'/knowdb')

In specifying the database, we create the directory (os.mkdir) where the database will reside (if necessary) and we will natively connect to the database. We use os.path.exists to check if the directory exists. Since we want the directory in the user's folder, and we have no way of knowing beforehand what this directory is, we use os.path.expanduser to replace / home/user as it would normally on the Unix console.

On line 11 of Specifying the database, we see the command that creates the connection to be used by all objects created in this module.

Next, we specify our database table as a class, in which its attributes are the table columns.

Specifying the database ideatable.

class Idea (SQLObject): name= UnicodeCol() nlinks= IntCol()

links= Pickle Col() address = StringCol

The class that represents our table is inherited from the SQLObject class. In this class, each attribute (table column) must be assigned an object that gives the type of data to be stored. In this example, we see four distinct types, but there are several others. UnicodeCol represents texts encoded as Unicode, i.e. it can contain characters from any language. IntCol is integer numbers. PickleCol is an exciting type as it allows you to store any type of Python object.

The most interesting thing about this type of column is that it does not require the user to invoke the pickle module to store or read this type of variable. Variables are automatically converted/converted according to the operation. Finally, we have StringCol which is a simpler version of UnicodeCol, accepting only ASCII character strings. In SQL it is common to have terms that specify different types according to the length of the text you want to store in a variable. In sqlobject, there is no limit to the size of the text that can be stored in either StringCol or UnicodeCol.

The functionality of our spider has been divided into two classes: Crawler, which is the creeper itself, and the UrlFac class that builds URLs from the word you want in Wikipedia.

Each page is pulled by the urllib2 module. The urlencode function of the urllib module makes it easy to add data to our request so as not to show that it comes from a digital spider. Without this disguise, Wikipedia refuses the connection.

The pages are then parsed by the VerResp method, where BeautifulSoup has a chance to do its work. Using the SoupStrainer function, we can find the rest of the document, which doesn't interest us, by analyzing only the links (tags 'a') whose destination is URLs beginning with the string/wiki/. All Wikipedia articles start this way. Thus, we avoid chasing external links. From the soup produced we extract only the URLs, i.e. what comes after "href =".

The Pickle Module

The pickle module and its fastest cPickle cousin implement algorithms that allow you to store Python-implemented objects in a file.

Example of using the pickle module

```python
import pickle

class hi:

  def say_hi (self):

    print " hi "

a= hi()

f= open ('pic test','w')

pickle.dump(a, f)

f.close()

f= open ('pic test','r')

b=pickle.load (f)

b.say_hi()

hi
```

As we see in the example of using the pickle module, with the pickle module we can store objects in a file, and retrieve it without problems for advanced use. However, an important feature of this module is not evident in example 8.1. When an object is stored using the pickle module, neither the class code nor its data are included, only the instance data.

```python
class hi:

  def say_hi (self, name=' alex'):
```

```
print'hi %s !'%name
```

```
f= open ('pictest','r')
```

```
b=pickle.load (f)
```

```
b.say_hi()
```

hi alex !

This way we can modify the class, and the stored instance will recognize the new code as it is restored from the file, as we can see above. This feature means that pickles do not become obsolete when the code they are based on is updated (of course this is only for modifications that do not remove attributes already included in the pickles).

The pickle module is not built for data storage, simply, but for complex computational objects that may contain data themselves. Despite this versatility, it is because it consists of a readable storage structure only by the pickle module itself in a Python program.

The SQLite3 Module

This module becomes part of the standard Python library from Version 2.5. Therefore, it becomes an excellent alternative for users who require the functionality of an SQL1-compliant relational database.

SQLite was born from a C library that had an extremely lightweight database and no concept client-server. In SQLite, the database is a file handled through the SQLite library.

To use SQLite in a Python program, we need to import the SQLite3 module.

import sqlite3

The following step is the creation of a connection object, through which we can execute SQL commands.

c= sqlite 3.connect (' /tmp/ example')

We now have an empty database consisting of the example file located in the / tmp directory. SQLite also allows the creation of RAM databases. To do this, simply replace the file name with the string: memory. To insert data into this database, we must first create a table.

c.execute ("" create table specimens (name text, real height, real weight)"")

< sqlite 3.Cursor object at 0 x83fed10 >

Note that SQL commands are sent as strings through the Connection object, execute method. The create table command creates a table; it must necessarily be followed by the table name and a list of typed variables (in parentheses), corresponding to the variables contained in this table. This command creates only the table structure. Each specified variable will correspond to one column of the table. Each subsequent entry will form a table row.

c.execute ("" insert into specimens values (' tom', 1 2.5, 2.3)"'

The insert command is another useful SQL command for inserting records into a table.

Although SQL commands are sent as strings over the connection, it is not recommended, for security reasons, to use the string formatting methods ('... values (% s,% s)'% (1,2)) of Python Instead, do the following:

t= (' tom',)

c.execute ('select from specimens where name=?', t)

c.fetch all()

[(' tom', 1 2.5, 2.2 9 9 9 9 9 9 9 9 9 9 9 9 9 9 9 8)]

In the example above we use the fetchall method to retrieve the result of the operation. If we wanted to get a single record, we would use fetchone.

Below is how to insert more than one record from existing data structures. In this case, it is a matter of repeating the operation described in the earlier example, with a sequence of tubes representing the sequence of records to be inserted.

t= ((' j e r r y', 5.1, 0.2), (' butch', 4 2.4, 1 0.3))

for i in t:

  c.execute (' insert into specimens value s (?, ?, ?)', i)

The cursor object can also be used as an iterator to get the result of a query.

c.execute (' selectfrom specimens by weight')

```
for reg in c:

 print reg
```

(' jerry', 5.1, 0.2)

(' tom', 1 2.5, 2.2 9 9 9 9 9 9 9 9 9 9 9 9 9 9 8)

(' butch', 4 2.4, 1 0.3)

The SQLite module is really versatile and useful, but it requires the user to know at least the rudiments of the SQL language. The following solution seeks to solve this problem in a more Pythonic way.

The SQLObject Package

The SQLObject2 package extends the solutions presented so far in two ways: it offers an object-oriented interface to relational databases, and also allows us to interact with multiple databases without having to change our code.

To exemplify sqlobject, we will continue to use SQLite because of its practicality.

Building a Digital Spider

In this example, we will have the opportunity to build a digital spider that will gather information from the web (Wikipedia3) and store it in an SQLite bank via sqlobject.

For this example, we will need some tools that go beyond the database. Let's explore the ability of the standard Python library to interact with the internet, and let's use an external package to decode the pages obtained.

The BeautifulSoup4package is a webpage breaker. One of the most common problems when dealing with Html pages is that many of them have minor design flaws that our browsers ignore, but can hinder further scrutiny.

Hence the value of BeautifulSoup: it is capable of handling faulty pages, returning a data structure with methods that allow quick and simple extraction of the desired information. Also, if the page was created using another encoding, BeautifulSoup, returns all Unicode content automatically without user intervention.

From the standard library, we will use the sys, os, urllib, urllib2 and re modules. The usefulness of each character becomes clear as we move forward in the example.

The first step is to specify the database. SQLObject allows us to choose from MySQL, PostgreSQL, SQLite, Firebird, MAXDB, Sybase, MSSQL, or ADODBAPI. However, as we have already explained, we will restrict ourselves to using the SQLite bank.

Chapter 11 Exception Handling

What exactly are exceptions? Why haven't we come across this so far? Well, we have, or at least you may have quite a lot of time but never noticed before. Create any program to make it crash deliberately.

Here's one that I created:

name = "Bruce Wayne"

age = 45

print(name + age)

Process finished with exit code 1

See the error? Not the one in the middle, I am referring to the very last line. It says the program ended with an exit code followed by the number one. That 'one' is informing us that something went wrong, and the program ended in a crash or abruptly ended. If the code were zero, it would have meant that our code went through and got executed beautifully!

We, as Python programmers, are bound to know when such errors are about to come. It's called anticipating, and it is something you should have already done when you say the first three lines of my latest code.

The problem is, we programmers would know what this code means. For any ordinary user, they would have no clue what this means and would end up searching YouTube libraries, just to find a video that explains what the error code 1 means. There is a way we can address this situation, and that is called exception handling.

Before we begin, just remember the bold text that says 'TypeError' on our error that occurred just a moment ago. We will need to recall that a little later.

Exception handling is where we tell a program to try a block of code and see if the same works fine. If not, anticipate the type of error you will get. Except for showing a console that is lit up with gibberish, we then tell Python to print out a user-friendly text that means something. Don't worry about the words 'try' and 'except' because that is exactly what I will be showing you now.

```
try:

name = "Bruce Wayne:"

age = 45

print(name + age)

except TypeError:

print("Please use a formatted string or convert age to a string")
```

We have just asked Python first to try a situation out. If the code is executed without returning any errors, it's fine. If not, it will type in a friendly message instead of letting the users know what to do to avoid this. This will prevent the application from crashing and keep users informed of the errors they may have made. Now, let's try and run this through to see what we get.

Please use a formatted string or convert age to a string

Process finished with exit code 0

Since we knew we were encountering a 'TypeError', we have just rectified the situation and now look; the program ended with an exit code of zero. Yay!

Here's something for you to know! The exception we created here only deals with a specific type of error. If this error were ValueError, the code would not execute, and the program will still crash.

Let us look at how that works as well, shall we?

try:

age = 45

age1 = 0

average = age / age1

print(average)

except TypeError:

print("Please use a formatted string or convert age to a string")

What do you think will happen here? Would the program go through? Would this program be able to catch the exception that might be caused, in case the program decides to crash? Let's find out.

Traceback (most recent call last):

File "C:/Users/Programmer/PycharmProjects/PFB/exception.py", line 4, in <module>

average = age / age1

ZeroDivisionError: division by zero

Process finished with exit code 1

That was expected. Since the exception caused here is different from the one we have created earlier on, it just went through and crashed. Time to put our thinking caps on and come up with an exception to handle this situation.

```
try:

age = 45

age1 = 0

average = age / age1

print(average)

except ZeroDivisionError:

print("For God's sake! Who divides a number with 0?")

except TypeError:
```

print("Please use a formatted string or convert age to a string")

What do you think now? Will this work, or will we still end up with an exit code of 1?

For God's sake! Who divides a number with 0?

Process finished with exit code 0

And that's how you do this! Now, everyone knows what went wrong and how they can correct the error they may have unintentionally caused.

It is something of a trait to have to be able to anticipate errors coming your way beforehand. It comes with practice, but it is certainly a trait to have for any programmer from any corner of the world.

The better you are at handling exceptions, the easier your users will find the program/application to use. They would know what needs to be done, how to sort matters out, and how to continue having a great experience while using your written programs.

Debugging, Exception Handling in Detail

Straight away, by classes, I do not mean the regular classes that you would expect at schools, colleges, and universities, nor do I mean that there are qualities of Python in any way; they are completely different things.

Classes are not exclusive to Python, but they are as important as anything else for any programmers across the globe. These are found in almost all known computer programming languages.

In the simplest definition, classes are what we use to define new types of data that we use. I did say there were three in the start, strings, numbers, and Booleans. Then we came across little more complex things called lists, tuples, and dictionaries. But what if you are still unable to get the desired outcome from the program you have been working on for such a long time? What if you feel like there must be something else apart from these types which can help you achieve greater results? Fortunately, classes are your answer.

A class can hold various functions and methods within itself. It does not need parentheses like functions and methods, nor do we create these by using the 'def' keyword. These are created using the word 'class', and they can be super helpful, especially for programmers with a keen interest in object-oriented programming.

Creating Our First Class

Before you even begin to create a class, or function, or any other kind of component, always visualize what you want to get out of it. It makes things a lot easier for you as a programmer.

At this point, you may be blank and might be struggling to come up with a class to create. Let me help you out with one. Let us create a class to which we want specific functions and methods attached to. We want this class to do things other data types were unable to do so.

I will not be creating anything that may fall outside the scope of this book, so what I have here is easily understandable. However, there are a few things that might take you by surprise, but those are deliberate so that you have every chance of understanding what they are.

```
class Instructor:

def __init__(self, name):

self.name = name

def talk(self):

print("talk")

me = Instructor("Keanu Reeves")

print(me.name)

me.talk()
```

The first thing to notice here is the naming convention I have used to name the class. Always use an uppercase for the first letter for every word that you may type when naming a class. You do not need to use underscores to separate words either. If you were to name this class as your first class, it would look like this:

```
class MyFirstClass
```

Next, we have the familiar 'def' keyword. But what about the double underscores and init? You may have already noticed these when calling methods. These are called constructors. For now, all you need to know is that we call upon these to initialize something.

Then, we have a parameter that says 'self', and I did not put it there. It is something that will come up automatically. It is referencing itself. We have only added another parameter called 'name' to allow us to use strings as names to display. Next, we gave the object an attribute called 'name', as seen above. Attributes are required to provide your functions a greater detail.

The following function is rather simple. We just created a function called to talk and asked Python to print out the same on the prompt.

Moving forward, or downwards by two spaces, we created a variable called 'me' with an assigned value of the class we just created. Notice how I have used class as a function (with parentheses). You might be wondering that I just said moments ago that classes do not need parentheses, and yet, I am using them here. When you are defining classes, you do not need these; however, when you are using them, you will need to rely on them to pass additional information.

Now, with the print command ready, I used my newly created class to call upon an attribute of '.name', which I created within this class. This then allows the prompt to print out the name, followed by the last function, which was again another print statement as defined above.

Classes are generally created so that other objects can be created using these classes. Imagine two characters, Tony and Steve. We want each of these to be objects carrying different attributes like name, age, and suit color. To do that, we will first need to create a class. Let us go ahead and do so.

```python
class Heroes:

    def __init__(self, name, age, color):

        self.name = name

        self.age = age

        self.color = color

    def introduce_self(self):

        print("My name is " + self.name)

        print(f"I am about {self.age} years old")

        print("My costume color is " + self.color)


hero1 = Heroes("Steve", 40, "Blue")

hero2 = Heroes("Tony", 38, "Red")

hero1.introduce_self()

hero2.introduce_self()
```

Output:

My name is Steve

I am about 40 years old

My costume color is Blue

My name is Tony

I am about 38 years old

My costume color is Red

We began by naming our classes appropriately. We then created a constructor to help us create various attributes that we can call upon later. Before doing so, ensure that you pass those as parameters after 'self' so that they are recognizable by the program interpreter. After defining attributes and assigning them values, we created a function called 'introduce_self' where we had three statements printed. Notice how the second one is a formatted string. That is because the age is an integer, and it will not work if you try to merge a string and an integer on their own.

Once sorted and happy, we moved on to create objects called 'hero1' and 'hero2' from the same class. Now, instead of typing this information separately, we just passed the information as arguments in the 'Heroes()' class. Next, we just ran a function we created earlier on, and the rest was just plain history.

I know this might be a little complicated at first. Classes are a subject that is normally apt for advanced students of Python. Still, it is essential that you, as a programmer, do not just stop thinking you know everything and miss out on some of the more advanced learning opportunities. Mastering classes will take quite a bit of time. Might not suffice to give you the perfect command of classes and some other aspects of programming. I intended to introduce you to this vast world of advanced topics. How you practice, and research on this is your call.

Chapter 12 Panda Python Data Analysis Library

This library is one of the best when it comes to machine learning and data science, and will stand for Python Data Library. According to many sources on this library, Pandas is going to be the name because it is derived from the term of panel data. This is basically an econometrics term that handles data sets that are multidimensional in structure.

Pandas are going to be seen as a bit game changer when it is time to analyze the data that you have using the Python language, and it is often going to be the number one Python library to use when it is time to handle data munging and wrangling. It can also handle all of the other aspects of data science that you want as well, making it an all in one library for your needs. Pandas are also going to be open-sourced, free for any programmer to use, and is one of the best data science libraries to focus on.

There are a lot of cool things that come with the Pandas library, so taking some time to look it over and figure out what it all entails will help you with a lot of data science projects. One thing that is cool with Pandas is that it is able to take almost any kind of data and will then create an object in Python with rows and columns. These are going to be called the data frame and it is going to look pretty much like what we see with Excel. If you have worked with the R programming language before, then you will see some similarities here as well.

However, compared to working with the dictionaries or lists that come with Python, or through loops or list comprehensions, the Pandas library is going to be so much easier overall. The different functions that come with Pandas can make it a much easier library to work with, especially when it comes to some of the complexities of working with data science.

Installing the Pandas Library

The following thing that we need to take a look at here is how to actually install the Pandas library and get it all set up. To install this library, we need to have a Python version that is at least 2.7 or higher. The Pandas library is not designed to work with any of the older versions of Python, so if you have one of the older versions, it may be time to upgrade. At this time, you need to make sure that some other deep learning libraries are in place. Pandas are going to be dependent on a few other libraries, based on what you would like to accomplish. It really needs to have at least NumPy associated with it, and if you want to do something like plotting with your information, then you need to work with Matplotlib.

Because you need a few extras that go with this library, we may want to consider installing a package to make sure that all the extras are there when you need them. The Anaconda distribution is a good option to work with and it can work on all of the major operating systems including Linux, OS X, and Windows systems.

Pandas is able to work with the Python IDE, including options like Spyder or the Jupyter Notebook. But to get these to work, the Pandas library has to be installed and ready to go. The Anaconda extension will come with both of the IDE or Integrated Development Environment, so that can make things easier to handle.

Importing one of these libraries means that you need first to load it into your memory, and once the installation is all done, you will be able to open up the needed files and work with them at any time. to make sure that you can import Pandas in the right manner, all that you need to do is run the following code below:

To make the codings easier, you can add second part (as pd) because it allows you to access Pandas with just the pd.command, rather than having to go through the process of writing out pandas.command each time that you wish to use it. As we can see with the code above as well, you need to import NumPy at this time. NumPy is a useful library to work with any scientific computing in Python, and often the Pandas library will need to pull out functions and other parts from this to get things done. At this point, Pandas is up and running and ready for us to use.

The Benefits of Using Pandas

With that work done, it is time to take a look at some of the many different benefits that come with using the Pandas library. There are a lot of benefits to this one, and it is one of the most popular options that come with this kind of data science work. With this in mind, let's take a look at some of the benefits that we are able to see with the Pandas library.

The first benefit that comes with the Pandas library is the data representation. Pandas are going to provide programmers with a streamlined form of data representation. This is going to be vital as you analyze and work to understand the data that you hold onto a bit better. When you can simplify some of the data representation that you have, it is going to facilitate better results for some of your projects in data science.

The second benefit of this library is that it provides us with a way to get more work done, without having to do as much writing. This is actually one of the most significant advantages that we are able to see with this library. With the traditional form of Python, we may have taken many lines of code to get the work done, without any support libraries, but with Pandas, we can get that same work done in just one or two lines of code. This means that by using Pandas, we are able to shorten up the procedure of handling the data that we have. When we can save all of that time, we are able to focus more on the algorithms that we need for the data analysis.

An extensive set of useful features is following on the list of Pandas benefits. Pandas are going to be seen as really powerful in the coding world. They are able to provide us with a big set of commands and features that are important, and which can be used to look through the data and analyze it quickly. We can use Pandas in order to perform various tasks including filtering out the data based on conditions that we set, or segregating and segmenting the data according to the preferences that we would like to meet.

The following benefit that comes with working with Pandas is that this library is able to handle a large amount of data in an efficient manner. When the Pandas library was initially been created, its goal was to handle large sets of data in an efficient manner. Pandas can really help us to save a lot of time and hassle because it is able to import large amounts of data quickly and efficiently.

The Pandas library is also able to make data customizable and flexible. There is a massive set of features in Pandas that can be applied to the data that you have. This can be great for beginners because it helps us to customize, edit, and pivot that data according to what we want to see happen. This is going to ensure that we can get the most out of our data each time.

And finally, the last benefit that we will see with the Pandas library is that it is made for Python. Python is one of the most prominent and most sought-after programming languages in the whole world, and it has an extensive amount of features that we can enjoy. And with just the amount of productivity that is offered, it is no wonder that many people want to learn how to code in this language.

Because of this, and all of the great features that come with Python, the fact that we are able to code with the help of Python in Pandas is going to be a great thing. It allows the programmer to tap into the power of many libraries and features that work with Python, which adds in some of the strength and power that we need with our coding.

Now, there are a few disadvantages that come with this library compared to some of the others, but often there are ways to work around these. Some of the disadvantages that can come with the Pandas library that programmers need to be aware of include:

The learning curve is steeper: Pandas was thought to have mild learning slow in the beginning. But the more that you explore the library, the steeper the learning curve is going to become. Sometimes the functionality of this library is going to get confusing, and for beginners, this is going to bring on some challenges.

The syntax can be hard: While Pandas is going to work with the Python language, sometimes it is going to add in some challenges when it comes to the syntax that has to be used. Switching back and forth between Python and Pandas codes can cause some problems

It doesn't work well with 3D matrices: If this is something that you want to work with, it can be a drawback of this library. If you are planning on just creating a 2D matrix, then this will not be a problem at all.

Wrong documentation: Without a right amount of documentation to go along with the project, it can be challenging to learn a new library. The documentation that comes in Pandas isn't going to do much to help us get the harder functions of the library done. This is going to slow down our learning procedure and can make coding difficult.

Viewing and Inspecting the Data

One thing that Pandas is able to do to help with our data science project is to work with viewing and inspecting the data. In reality, Pandas is able to help with all of the various processes that you may want to do with data science, but right now we are just going to focus on this part. You can use a variety of the functions that come with Pandas in order to take a look at what is in the data, figure out if there are any missing or duplicate values, and then make the changes as needed to work on your data analysis.

With this in mind, it is also possible for us to get some statistics on the entire series, or an entire data frame. Some of the codes that you would need to use to make this happen includes:

Df.mean(): This one is going to help us return the mean of all our presented columns.

Df.corr(): This one is going to return the correlation between the columns that are in your frame of data.

Df.std(): This one is going to help us see what the standard deviation ends up being between each of the columns.

Df.median(): This one is going to help us see what the median of each column is like.

Df.min(): This one is going to help us see the lowest value that is present in each of our columns.

Df.max(): This one is going to help us see the highest value in each of our columns.

Df.count(): This one is going to help us by returning the number of all of the non-null values that show up in each column of the data frame we are using.

Conclusion

Thank you for making it to the end of Machine Learning with Python. Let us hope that it was informative and able to provide you with all of the tools you need to achieve your goals whatever they may be. The objective of this is to present an introduction for the absolute beginners to machine learning and data science

This covers the dominant machine learning paradigms, namely supervised, unsupervised, semi-supervised, and reinforcement. This explains how to develop machine learning models in general and how to develop a neural network which is a particular method of performing machine learning. It teaches how to train and evaluate their accuracy.

Python is a widely used programming language for different applications and in particular for machine learning. This covers the basic Python programming as well as a guide to use Python libraries for machine learning.

This presents machine learning applications using real datasets to help you enhance your Python programming skills as well as machine learning basics acquired through the book. These applications provide examples of developing a machine learning model for predictions using linear regression, a classifier using logistic regression and artificial neural network. Through these applications, examples of data exploration and visualization using Python are presented.

Nowadays, machine learning is used in every domain, such as marketing, health care systems, banking systems, stock market, gaming applications, among others. This book's objective is to provide a basic understanding of the significant branches of machine learning as well as the philosophy behind artificial neural networks. This also aims at providing Python programming skills for machine learning to beginners with no earlier programming skills in Python or any other programming language.

Remember that deep learning is relatively easy, contrary to collective thinking among programmers. The industry is quickly moving toward the top to take control of machines. There are lots of people who are firmly in favor of machine learning, but I have some solid reasons that deep learning is more profitable than machine learning. Practically speaking, deep learning is a subset of machine learning. It secures power and flexibility by learning the world on the basis of the database that it has stored in the backend.

It works on the back of its hidden learning architecture that consists of multiple layers with some dense layers. The data is processed through these layers where the neural networks get to work on matching the input data with the data that is stored in the databases in the backend. Upon each match, they return the output on the basis of some highly educated findings that are efficient and very well managed.

Once you have acquired the skills and understood the reasoning behind machine learning models presented in this book, you will be able to use these skills to solve complex problems using machine learning. You will also be able to easily acquire other skills and use more advanced machine learning methods. In this guide, I explained to you the basics of Python language. Learning to program is like learning another language. It takes a lot of patience, study, application, method, passion and above all perseverance.

What I can suggest is to do as much practice as possible by starting to rewrite the hundreds of examples you find in this guide. Try to memorize them and when you write the code, say it to yourself, in your mind (open bracket, close round brackets and so on). In the beginning, this helped me a lot to memorize better the various steps needed to write a program even if simple.

It is important not to feel like heroes when a program works but above all you should not be depressed when you cannot find a solution to your programming problems. The network is full of sites and blogs where you can always find a solution.

I hope that this guide has been useful for you in learning Python.